The Beginning of an End

A Chronicle on Kabul's Fall:
From What Was Seen and Heard

By: Abdul Qahar Asi
Translated by: Nima Asi

Form Publications | نشر فرم

The Beginning of an End

A Chronicle on Kabul's Fall: From What Was Seen and Heard

By: Abdul Qahar Asi
Translated by: Nima Asi

Editor: Faramin Michael & Farid Barzgar
Cover Design: A. Evelyn
First edition : 2024, Norway
Number of prints: Unlimited
ISBN: 4-00-94106-82-978

www.formbook.org
info@formbook.org

About the Author:

Abdul Qahar Asi, a distinguished poet , was born on September 28, 1956, in the idyllic Panjshir Province of Afghanistan. At the tender age of five, his family relocated to Kabul. After completing his secondary education, he gained admission to the Faculty of Agriculture at Kabul University.
Renowned as one of Afghanistan's most gifted poets of the late 1980s, Asi composed all his works in his native Persian language. Throughout his lifetime, he published six collections of both modern and classic poetry. His verses were so exceptional that numerous singers, most notably the celebrated musician and singer Farhad Darya, crafted songs from Asi's patriotic and romantic poems. His first prose work, "The Beginning of an End," was initially published in Iran.
Tragically, Asi's life was cut short in 1994 during Mujahideen's civil war in Kabul when a rocket struck him, ending the journey of a poet whose words had touched countless hearts.

Table of Contents:

- The collapse of Khost Province and the metal trade
- The Stories of Ibrahim
- Insulting women
- Attack on Hindu (Sikh) minority and their properties
- My observations
- Some short but worth reading tales…
- The end
- Silent, Sir!

Acknowledgement

The Taliban's capture of Kabul on August 15, 2021, is reminiscent of several earlier collapses in Afghanistan's history. In July 1973, Dawood Khan, posing as the country's first president, launched a white coup against his cousin, King Zahir Shah, putting an end to the last Afghanistan Monarchy finding the first-ever republic and becoming the first president of the country. Five years later, in April 1978, the communists struck the presidential palace, resulting in the death of Dawood Khan and his whole family. This event in the nation's contemporary history is known as the Communist Coup. The Red Army subsequently invaded Afghanistan, which infuriated the youth, who saw it as an invasion by The Union of Soviet Socialist Republics (USSR). They ascended the Afghan mountains and rebelled against the Red Army, using the name Mujahideen. The Red Army and the Mujahideen engaged in combat until 1989 when communist Russia chose to withdraw its forces from Afghanistan. Even after leaving Afghanistan, Russia maintained its support to Najibullah, the final communist president; nonetheless, Najibullah was unable to withstand pressure from the Mujahideen, who were determined to take total control of Afghanistan. As a result,

Najibullah, Afghanistan's last communist president, resigned, making room for the Mujahideen to take over Kabul.

In 1992, internal conflicts among Mujahideen factions led to a devastating civil war in Afghanistan. This conflict caused significant migrations—both legal and illegal—and resulted in extensive destruction in Kabul, claiming thousands of lives. Among those killed was Qahar Asi, a renowned Afghan poet who died from a mortar strike while walking with friends, having returned from Iran just days before. During his time in Iran, Asi experienced the same challenges as other Afghan migrants, such as harsh treatment by authorities, financial struggles, and the pain of being separated from his family in Kabul. Despite his literary accomplishments, he was never recognized as a distinguished poet seeking refuge.

My late uncle (Abdul Qahar Asi) was killed nearly a year before my birth. Reading Asi's collections of poetry as a child made me aware of my obligation to translate them into English, but I was never able to do so. However, after the fall of Kabul in the hands of the Taliban, I began to translate his chronicle, 'The Beginning of an End', which describes the fall of Najibullah's USSR-led government and the rise of the Mujahidin in Kabul on April 28, 1992.

The Beginning of an End was initially published (1996) in Iran after Asi died in 1994. Considering that he had previously published six collections of poetries, his journal of the Mujahideen era is regarded as his only prose. In contrast to his prose, which opposes warlords and the Mujahideen, critics claim that Asi frequently discusses beauty, love, and patriotism in his poetry. Indeed, under Afghanistan's communist government (1979–1989), Asi used to often praise the Mujahideen in his poetry. The Mujahideen, however, manifested themselves to act against all the values that Asi stood for. Meanwhile, some other critics argue that his memoir stems from his sense of guilt for having praised the Mujahideen commanders, who made Asi and many others leave Kabul immediately after they took power.

Since the Taliban took back control on August 15, 2021,

people have inevitably been witnessing the same catastrophe that they experienced when Najibullah's government fell in 1992. Asi wrote his chronicle in opposition to the crimes committed by the Mujahideen in 1994 a few months before he was killed. However, if he were still living today, I think he would have written a book titled The Resumption of an End: A Report on the Never-ending Fall of Kabul from 1992–2021. Of course, it would have been a thick book. Unfortunately, the fact is that he is no longer with us, but I believe that The Beginning of an End, his book that recounts a brief moment in real history, will be read by a wider audience. So, the readers need to identify the resemblance between the fall of Kabul in 2021 and 1992 as they read all the real, tragic stories that happened to Qahar Asi and the rest of the residents of Kabul in a beginning that has never had an end to it so far.

Nima Asi,
10.05.2023

Key Words:

1. Najibullah: The last president of the communist regime in Afghanistan. His government was overthrown by the Mujahideen factions.
2. Maidan and Wardak: Used to be Two separate provinces located in the west of Kabul. Now they are both in one province called Maidan-Wardak.
3. Snuff/Naswar: A narcotic drug made from tobacco. It is put in the mouth and its users in Afghanistan spit it out after a few minutes. The tobacco in it targets the tiny nerves within the mouth.
4. Kabul River: This passes through Kabul City and is often dry or polluted with sewage.
5. Makrorayan Block Apartments: A complex of residential apartments in the east of Kabul. The residential blocks were built by the USSR-appointed government.
6. Pishawari Leaders: The author refers to the Mujahedeen leaders who lived and directed Afghanistan from Peshawar province of Pakistan. Meaning that they were receiving their orders from Pakistani leaders.
7. Pashtuns: One of the ethnic groups in Afghanistan.
8. Dal and Chapati: Famous and common food types

in Pakistan.

9.   The Silent Soldier: A pamphlet containing some appealing facts about the Afghan Jihadi leaders, published in Pakistan.

10.   Watan Party: The new name of a Marxist Party established by Najibullah.

11.   Takhar: A province in the northeast of Afghanistan.

12.   Pashtunism: The author was informed about Najibullah's Pashtunist affiliations by Sayed Hamidullah. The term refers to chauvinism that Pashtun leaders represent which is the superiority of a specific ethnic group over other ethnic groups in Afghanistan.

13.   Khalq and Parcham: Two Marxist Parties that were supported by the USSR-led government. Both parties had disputes on some political arguments in Afghanistan. Both parties' leaders governed Afghanistan.

14.   Hazara: One of the marginalized ethnic groups in Afghanistan.

15.   Gulbudin Hekmatyar: The leader of the Islamic Party made up of most Pashtun members.

16.   Afghan Film: The Governmental Directory of the Afghan Film Industry, is an institution under the Ministry of Information and Culture.

17.   Nabi Azimi: One of the former generals of the communist regime who had previously served as the Minister of Defense.

18.   Ahmad Shah Masoud: One of the Mujahideen leaders in Afghanistan. According to the Peshawar agreement, he was chosen as the minister of defence by the Mujahedin Leaders in Peshawar.

19.   Sibghatullah Mujaddedi: Intern President of the Mujahideen in Afghanistan after overtaking the government from Najibullah.

20.   Durand Line/Border: Refers to the borderline between Afghanistan and Pakistan. The Durand Line was established in 1893 as the international border between the Emirate of Afghanistan and the Indian Empire by Mortimer Durand, a British diplomat of the Indian Civil Service, and Abdur Rahman Khan, the Emir of Afghanistan, to fix the limit of their respective spheres of influence.

11   The Beginning of an End

Kabul and the Regime Before the Collapse

The situation of Kabul citizens

Before the Mujahedin took over Kabul, the city was on the edge of an economic collapse. The trading roads of other provinces of Afghanistan leading to the capital, Kabul, were destroyed, and the so-called Russian aid was brought in through the air (by planes). Also, during the last three years of the presidency of Najibullah, most of the developing and constructive projects were not active, which caused many troubles for people, particularly government workers, and made them live in constant financial chaos. The families were so much in financial trouble that, sometimes, one person was not just in charge of one but four or five families whose brothers and sisters were killed (martyred) and needed help from others.

Electricity was bought from Mujahidin commanders, so-called (Ghazi) a term which refers to Muslims who kill non-Muslims, particularly in War. This means some Mujahidin fighters who had command of electricity lines outside the cities were paid for not destroying power supplies that carried electricity to Kabul. It seems it was an old deal between Afghan Communist Leaders and the Mujahidin commanders to provide electricity for the poor Afghans who were supposed to use it in turns.

Less-paid governmental workforce having average salaries of 10,000 AFN, who were not given their benefits as well, were the most vulnerable ones, who could not even afford to buy 7/5k flour for 48,000 AFG; one loaf of bread for 150 AFG; and four litres of diesel for 2,500 AFG. Most of them chose to have a second income source such as being a vendor—after their official time in the afternoons. I knew two people who had two distinctive jobs: an expert in the Ministry of Technology and Communications who had to work as a porter; and a poet who also sold potatoes on Kabul streets.

The neighbourhoods in old Kabul City (central Kabul) had turned into the birthplace of diseases: burble and malaria had already spread and shattered the city. Diseases emerging due to a lack of food caused deaths and sent dead bodies to the Shuhada-e-Salehin (Righteous Martyrs) Cemetery in Kabul every day. In some cases, Haram meat was brought to Kabul from Maidan and Wardak cities and found by the Kabul security forces.; That is not the only case; even dead bodies of donkeys and dogs were sent to Kabul to be sold to people. (The meats were traded in from Maidan and Wardak provinces, where Mujahidin had control. Donkey and dog meat is considered Haram in Islam. Muslims are supposed to butcher animals in certain ways to make sure their meat is Halal, In this case, Haram means even goats and caws were not butcher properly or dead animals were traded to make money)

Many people came from the surrounding neighbourhoods or other cities to Kabul and started to build houses for themselves wherever they could without municipal approvals. Most of these houses were located in "Deh Kepak" in the north and "Poul Artal (The Artel Bridge)" in the centre of Kabul. Some other people started to build arbitrary houses on the hill sides of the "Sher Darwaza" and "Asamaie" mountains, which were and still are called "Zorabad" meaning

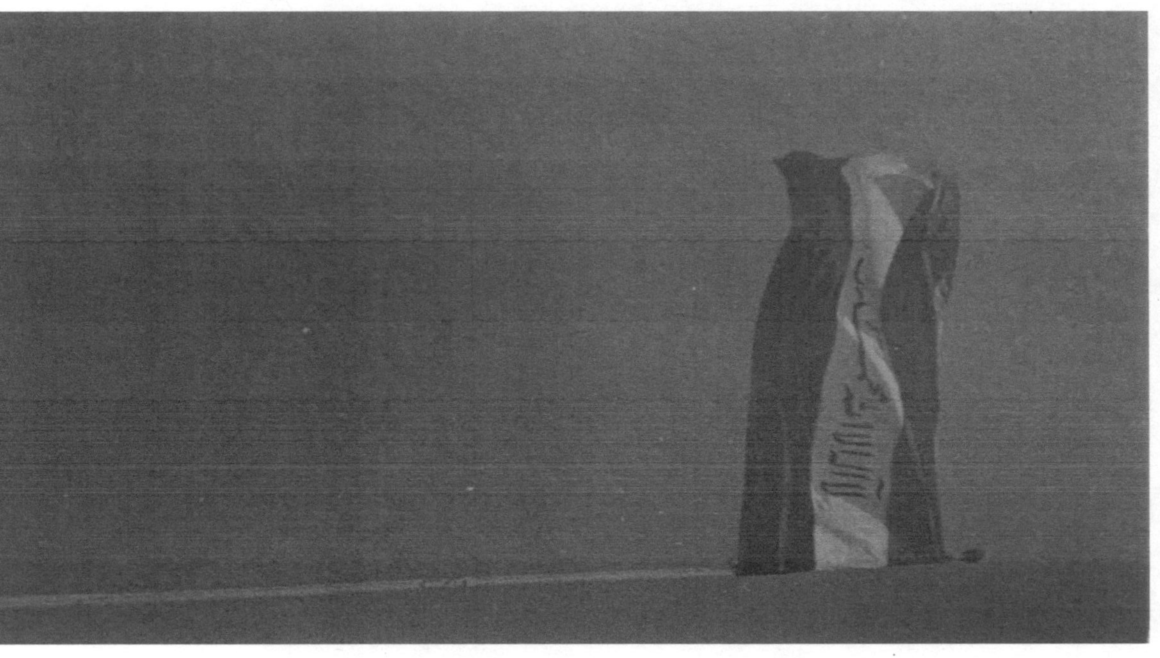

15 The Beginning of an End

build by force. If they were stopped by the municipal workers during the day, the people would persist and continue
construction at night due to the need for shelter—some of
these shelters looked like prehistoric caves. uConstruction
materials used in houses built in Zorabad were taken from
an ancient wall in Kabul that was considered one of the pre-
cious symbols that dated to the pre-Islamic period of the city.
The wall, which had more than a thousand years of history,
had been built on the peak of a mountain, but the lowbrow
army destroyed it in a way as if it were not there. Particularly
the parts of so called Kasa Burj / Bowl Tower and its extend-
ed strip. According to Engineer Shakib, former Director of
Historical Monuments of Afghanistan, the area of "Ghazni
Minaret", which was built during the Ghaznawi reign in the
Ghazni Province of Afghanistan hundreds of years ago and
is now considered a historic and valuable phenomenon, has
been changed into a living site by people, and from the clay
used in the buildings around the Ghazni Minaret, they make
bricks and other construction materials. If these self-evoked
buildings are not stopped, the Ghazni Minaret" will soon become some commander's property or appear in the middle of
a residential house built arbitrarily.

People were bringing their house items and selling them in
the second-hand market at half price to buy food and survive.
To buy bread, people had to line up in front of the bakeries for
hours. They were sending their children to the bakeries because—children could and had to wait until noo while their
elders had to go to do low-priced work. One winter morning
in 1989, two streets down from where I lived, a five-year-old
kid who, despite having pneumonia, had to wait in front of
a bakery where more than 70 people had already stood in
line to buy bread, was dead due to cold. He was found fro-
zen dead sitting with his head on his knees while it was his
turn to buy bread. Tales were told in the same winter that a
woman who got sick and died three days after she stood long
hours to buy bread for her children in a queue full of people.

The cultural situation was not better either. A wide range of
shows of popcorn movies in cinemas and cafes, and public

sale of hashish, snuff, and other illegal drugs had a great deal of heat in Kabul. I have seen plenty of drug addicts on the back alleys and byroads and what they call the "Kabul River", which runs through the middle of the city and was turned into the core of drug dealers and heroin addicts.

Hundreds of lepers were selling small mirrors, scissors, needles, etc. in different central areas of Kabul city, such as "Pul-e-Bagh Umumi", and Mandawi, and over the bridge on the opposite side of Saray Shahzada. The number of these people increased after the Mujahidin took over Kabul. The most vulnerable people were those who fought for the communist regime and became disabled (war disabled), but the regime did nothing despite promising them help in its slogans. Towards the end of Najibullah's presidency, to have houses of their own, some of the people with disabilities in Kabul invaded a few of the Makrorayan apartments (Russian-built residential blocks in the south of Kabul) for a few hours, but then they were forced out of the place. This incident is called "The Uprising of the Leglesses."

However, cultural associations and organizations were playing the role of a democratic and open-minded society through having publications of their own that, if they continued that way, might be quite effective and instrumental in intellectualism and liberalization.

In short terms, indeed it was Kabul's and its peoples' life. Among all those people, some of them were financially supported by their family members abroad: the U.S., European countries, Australia, and Iran. I think only these groups of people, whether abroad in Pakistan, Iran, and northern neighbouring countries or in the country, lived a somewhat comfortable life during the USSR's shameful invasion and after their fall during the Mujahidin reign.

Despite all the hardships, there was something to be happy about, and that was hope for the Kabul citizens: a regime that was not able to provide them food, safety and security would fall, and the rightful Mujahidin would gain victory.

The regime and its political struggles

An analysis of the situation after the collapse in Kabul would be impossible without assessing the position of the regime on the edge of collapse and Najibullah's political efforts that could smartly maintain his power and continue his regime for three more years after the USSR left Afghanistan. Without a doubt, Mujahidin leaders' incompetence and Najibullah's acuteness in political games were the causes behind the continuation of his regime. Najibullah had the exact perception of the Mujahidin opposition leaders. Now I shorten my paragraph by inserting one of Najibullah's speeches broadcasted on Afghanistan Radio Television on the Solar New Year's Night in March 1992/1371:

"We aspire to the participation of opposition forces in power, but the Peshawari leaders do not want this. Now, it doesn't matter if I remain in power, what matters is that if I resign, there will be a power vacuum, and I must say here that vacuum will bring war into Kabul City, and then there will be bloodshed district by district, street by street, and house by house. Current relative security will be disrupted, and none of them (the Mujahidin leaders) are capable of leading the country or bringing peace. I don't know if I would be dead or alive by then, but people should bear in mind that the leaders of the opposition don't have the capacity and effectiveness to create a powerful central government."

Indeed, from what Najibullah said, this one has been cemented in the minds of all the people who watched him and know that the remarks by him (Najibullah), who precisely knew his political and military rivals, are unforgettable. From the remarks, it is illuminated that this man, through his career in Afghanistan's intelligence agency, known as "Governmental Information and Service", also as the President of Afghanistan, could access the most accurate information about Jihadi Leaders in Afghanistan. Others' perceptions, including those of educated people, well-read analysts, and intellectuals, were so emotion-orientated, clumsy, and superficial that they thought of the word "power vacuum" in his speech as Naijibullah scrambled towards the preservation of his power.

In another speech addressing high-ranking military officials, Najibullah emphasized creating some type of understanding and coordination with the fighting fronts (Mujahidin) and, in a prediction, he foretold the future of Afghanistan and talked about the positive judgment of history about them (military soldiers and officials). However, no one had the same deep perception as he did, so no one took him seriously.

Najibullah had neither miracles nor genius. He came to those conclusions after having received evidence-based information. That is why he usually insisted on sharing power reasoning that the leaders who could not reach a common understanding about Islam in 14 years, would never make a united leadership and government; that is why he used to mock and talk of the wars (by the Mujahidin) in Jalalabad, Paktia, Logar, and other provinces, as well as the wars in areas surrounding Kabul such as Paghman and other areas. He condemned the presence of foreign fighters amongst the Mujahidin forces and defended himself as the one who, as he put it, "was independently ruling after making USSR forces leave the country". Although he committed various atrocities himself during those wars, he managed to govern and defend his presence despite the absence of Russians, and that was to his credit. He was the one who was in touch with some Mujahidin leaders, as he used to say, he had deals with some of them, which turned out be to true after the Mujahidin took power.

Najibullah was not reluctant to come into an agreement with the Mujahidin leaders and share power with them, so, on the one hand, he could have partial power and, on the other, would gain historical credit for having gathered fighting fronts around himself. Then, he would disappear dramatically from the political scene by actually defeating his rivals. He had an interesting plan for himself, but what interrupted his plans from being executed were the three main dilemmas that he had with three important parties including Jihadi Leaders, Jihadi Commanders, and his opponents in the government and the ruling party.

1. Najibullah's Dilemma with Jihadi Leaders

Najibullah's dilemma was not with the Mujahidin Leaders themselves; his concern was, that if he reconciled with them, he would have to accept being under the control of leader-making militants from another country (Pakistan). He appeared more Pashtun in this respect than the others, to the point that while Peshawari Leaders would say "yes," to their Pakistani superiors he wouldn't. It means that he respected his dignity and didn't like to accept leader-making militant dictations (he had been once dictated to by USSR Marshals and would not accept to lower his reputation to accept it now from Pakistanis), which is why generals behind (southern) borders were not happy with his presence in power in Afghanistan, otherwise it was like cutting a cake for Pakistani leaders to make their fellow Jihadi leaders to accept the deal.

After all, Najibullah, above all other pieces of evidence, had studied the "Silent Soldier" pamphlet, which was published in Pakistan and had an exposing subject about the Jihad in

Afghanistan. He knew about the shameful plans concerning the destruction of his country from the pamphlet. That is why his problems with Jihadi leaders had roots in the dictatorship of the leader-making generals. In summary, those generals could not find their interest in Najibullah's government as they invested and raised others for this purpose. To bring the people they wanted into power was not possible under the same ambirla with Najibullah and they could not agree on it. Because as mentioned earlier, Najibullah was prouder than Jihadist Leaders to receive orders from Pakistan.

2. Najibullah's Dilemma with the Jihadi Commanders in Afghanistan

Najibullha was very interested in reaching an understanding with Jihadi commanders, but his great wish and desire never came true. He fantasized about coming to terms with the greatest of them Ahmad Shah Masood. Abdul Hamid Muhtat, Vice President of Najibullah's government, and Farid Ahmad Mazdak, member of the Political Bureau and Deputy of Watan Political Party, have repeatedly quoted this from Najibullah to me. Muthat, at his home in the old Markrorayan settlement, quoted from Najibullah: "I only count on Masood, and I want to talk to him about resolving the country's. (Kabul's citizens themselves witnessed that the Ministry of Defense was vacant for Ahmad Shah Masood for months), but Masood seemed to be his games which indeed was smart on it.

According to Farid Ahmad Mazdak, in 1991, Najibullah had been trying hard to negotiate with Ahmad Shah Masood indirectly because if he entered into direct negotiations with him, Najibullah's rivals in his party, Watan, and the government would accuse him of being a spy who worked for the Mujahidin. According to himself, Muhtat had met Masood in the northern province of Takhar, which had taken place without any coordination with the presidency (Najibullah) in 1989, which caused disputes between Najibullah and Muhtat as well. But as I know Muhtat, he has always been curious and careful of himself and his life, and I certainly believe that he was either sent by the Russians or the president himself

for a mission.

Mr. Mahbubullah Koshani, president of "Revolutionary Organization of the Toilers of Afghanistan" known as (SAZA), told me of his meetings with Masood in 1988 and 1989 as being independent and without coordination with Najibullah (however, I doubt it). Everybody knows that his organization was directly made and led by the ruling government to run their visibility efforts including ideas around democracy, diversity and the existence of political parties and their publication.

If he had the chance, Najibullah had two tactical and strategic purposes for embracing Masoud. First, to have command on the largest opposing fighting front and secondly to destroy Jamiat-e-Islami, whose leadership was mostly of Tajik ethnicity who speak Farsi. Both plans were among the nationalist yet anti-Farsi strategies of Najibullah.

He considered his accounts clear with others according to his speech, which was broadcast on Kabul Radio Television in 1990, he was in contact with almost 60% of Jihadi commanders, such as "Mohammad Anwar Dangar", "Baqi Mohammad Anwar Jigdalik", "Mullah Ezat", "Karim Qarabaghi", "Mualem Fateh", and "Abdulhaq". Of course, we counted this among his exaggerations and regarded it as part of his boasting and naivety, because partisans like "Akbari", "Anwari" and "Sayed Jagran" in central Afghanistan; "Basir Khalid", "Sayed Najmuddin Wasiq", "Haqjo", "Arbab Hafiz" and "Ustad Farid" in the north; "Ismail Khan", "Mullah Nasim Akhunzada", "Mawlawi Naqibullah", "Qari Baba", "Mawlawi Jalaluddin Haqqani" etc., in the west, south-western, and south of Afghanistan could have a huge influence in events happening in the country in their way and term and they were not included within the 60% that he was referring. I think that Najibullah had no problem with his Pashtun opposition among Jihadis, given his Pashtunist affiliations, and was hoping to deal with them. This perception was confirmed by himself when he sent a message through his senior bodyguard, Sayed Hamidullah, to Ahmad Shah Masood after Mujahidin came to Kabul while he was a captive in the United Nations Country Office in Kabul. According to Sayed Hamidullah (he told me himself), Najibullah had advised Masood (through that message) to pay the commanders who are likely to accept it and reference his own experience of dealing with commanders during his presidency.

3.Najibullah's dilemma with his opponents within the government and the party

The third dilemma is firstly rooted in contradictions that initially appeared as "Khalq" (the Democratic People's Party of Afghanistan) and "Parcham" (the Flag of the People's Democratic Party of Afghanistan"), from the party which was supported by the USSR and later they expanded into forms of ethnicity, nationality, and language. The internal disputes went further to the extent that individuals like "Saleh Mohammad Zeray", a member of the People's Democratic Party of Afghanistan (Khalq) who was known as someone who made fun of mispronouncing Quran terms in party meetings, established a political fraction and, Sulaiman Layeq, another key member of that party, started having membership in every other party.
Members of the People's Democratic Party of Afghanistan (Khalq) were mostly Pashtuns and thought of themselves as the real executors of Moscow's communist plans, and it was easy for them to accept every strategy made by Moscow. They made fun of the members of The Flaq's Party of Afghanistan and called them "round-foot", accused them of being from the high class, and tried to expose their old relationship with Afghanistan's former royal family (which was true because, besides members of The Flag's Party being from the high class, they had cooperated when Dawood Khan, the first president of Afghanistan and the last leader from the Mohammad Zai family, who revolted against the Monarchy during the coup on July 16, 1973). Members of "The Flag's Party" called their rival, (the People's Democratic Party of Afghanistan), "dirty collars", whereas they were called "washed-up or soaped-up fishes by the other party (Khalq). Despite all of those internal conflicts, both parties were involved in crimes and destruc-

tions in the country equally, which would be enough for us to recall their collective murders in "Pul-e-Charkhe Prison" in Kabul and the rest of the prisons in Kunar, Herat, Badakhshan, and other provinces of Afghanistan; last but not least, they were the main cause behind death and disability of three and half million people in Afghanistan.

Najibullah was a smart member of "The Flag of the People's Democratic Party of Afghanistan" who was an intelligent, artistic type speaker and an emotional nationalist, which his last characteristic caused many tensions in his party. Once, we witnessed that he rejected a gift from people living in north Kabul, whose native language is Farsi. The reason given was that their sons (Mujahidin) had closed the Shamali/northern highway.

Farid Ahmad Mazdak once said: Once I was supposed to consult Najibullah to select the director of the "Youth's Association of Afghanistan", whomever I named, Najibullah asked me about his ethnicity. Another day, I chose a different approach and introduced three people to him based on their place of birth, naming their provinces as Kabul, Parwan, and Logar. Then he paused on the one who was from Logar, a province with the majority of Pashtuns, and asked for further details about him."

With his nationalist affiliations, Najibullah was positioned in a situation where all other ethnicities were claiming their lost rights. People from the Hazara ethnicity did not accept being discriminated against and humiliated anymore, and neither did the Uzbeks accept being blindly the servants of anyone anymore.

Accordingly, the pro-Pushtonism of Najibullah in military control of northern provinces by General Achok weakened the collaboration spirit of non-Pushton military forces such as General Momen in Hairatan and Uzbek forces under the command of General Dostum in Maza-e-Sharif. Instead, they come up with some kind of understanding against the government and gradually become rebels.

Another issue that enhanced other ethnic groups' unity was that Najibullah accelerated the process of settling Pashtun tribes in the north of Afghanistan to Pashtunize those areas. At the same time, Achok started to distribute thousands of hectares of people's land to Pashtun tribes with a chip price in Mazar-e-Sharifwhich awakened a long complex among northern residents of Afghanistan, as well as making General Momen and others disagree with Achok's mission in the north of Afghanistan and revolt against the regime. The revolutionary motivation had also found its way among governmental officials such as General Asif Dilawar, the Deputy Defense Minister, and Farid Ahmad Mazdak, who partly acted in favour of Najibullah's opponents. (e.g., G. Asif Dilawar had paved sanctuaries near Bagram airbase for the Jamiat-e-Islami forces, and Farid Ahmad Mazdak had also ordered the northern (governmental) forces to join Ahmad Shah Masoud's forces and persist against Najibullah when needed.

Activation of nongovernmental organizations and associations, lack of authority and role of law at every governmental level, the unstable position of international political and economic supporters of the regime, collapse of governmental administrative and military units in the provinces (of Afghanistan), the poor economic situation in Kabul, administrative corruption, and fatal bureaucracy put hands together and made the president and his team disparate and created chaos... What seemed strange was that, despite all of these abnormalities, the president wanted to have a self-centred position in reconciliation with his opposition (leaders).
Meanwhile, the disputes between senior leaders within the ruling party (Watan) and the president arose up to the general secretariate and according to Farid Ahmad Mazdak, the president constantly criticised the leakage of classified information to Ahmad Shah Masoud and he meat it was done by Farid Ahamd Mazdak and Najmuddin Kawiyani.

Backgrounds of the Collapse

In early 1992, Mazar-e-Sharif went completely out of the control of Najibullah's administration through an understanding with Mujahiddinand in the new solar year a delegation was sent by the president to handle the situation the they could not reach an agreement and returned empty-handed. Najibullah showed so much resistance against Achok's rivals (in the north) that he once said, "I will plant an Achok on each Uzbek's body. He even did not accept to appoint "Bheegi", who was a regime's experienced general because he was Uzbek to replace Achok. (Militant commanders in the north had proposed this that Najibullah))

Political and racial factors divided the government leaders into fractions. Farsi-speaking and other ethnicities went to Ahmad Shah Masoud, and Pashtuns went to Gulbuddin Hekmatyar.

After Balkh collapsed and Fahim, Ahmad Shah Masoud's envoy to Mazar-e-Sharif, went there, the political atmosphere in the north of Afghanistan changed. Masoud's forces advanced to Parwan province; General Rafi, Naib's envoy met with Hekmatyar and admired Hekmatyar on Kabul Television for the first time; multiple trips of foreign secretary of the regime to Parwan and his meeting with Ahmad Shah Masoud; Benin Siwan, the UN's special representative's busy schedule in Kabul and his five articles proposed solution the collapse of Baghlan, Samangan, and some other provinces in the north on the hands of Mujahidin, were the reasons that Najibullah felt he cannot continue as president. Accordingly, with the help of the UN's envoy, in early March 1992, Najibullah decided to leave the country and leave the Arg behind. But General Dostum's forces, who controlled Kabul Air-Port at the time, did not allow him to leave the country. They had told him that he must pay for his deeds to the people of Afghanistan. So Najibullah was taken to the UN envoy's office in Kabul. Having already sent his family to India, Najibullah remained in Kabul under UN protection, the page turned and Kabul collapsed.

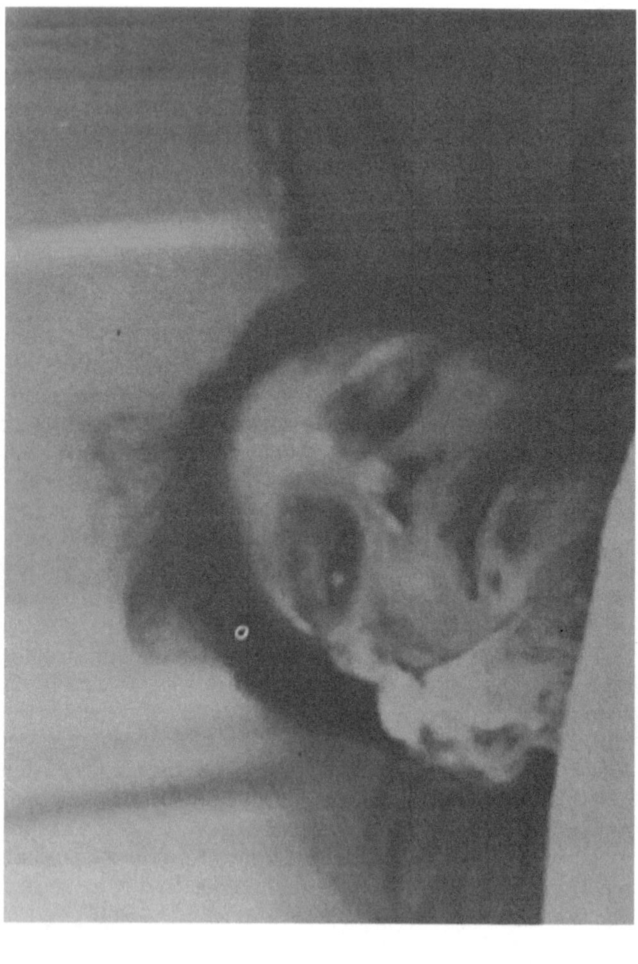

On the verge of collapse

During the early days of Mujahidin's presence in Kabul, and the opening of transportation blockages and cross roads between the capital and other provinces, and the new comers (Mujahiddin) were warmly welcomed by people in Kabul Those citizens whose financial situation was better than others began to provide charity by sacrificing sheep (a tradition in Afghanistan when people celebrate something they regard), and the poor citizens of Kabul were prying, thanking Almighty Allah for the communist regime having been defeated by the Mujahidin; those whose sons and loved ones had been killed during the communist revolution in Afghanistan began to forget the past and look for a bright future, allowing real Islamic forgiveness to flow in their hearts.

However, there were many concerning speculations exchanged among people in Kabul indicating an unpleasant future was about to come. Some speculations were made that Najibullah had sent along with his family thirteen strongboxes of government wealth through the air, with the boxes marked as highly classified as no one in the Kabul Airport was allowed to check and search them in the airport. It was said that Gulbuddin Hekmatyar's fraction wasas in charge of all police units in Kabul city, and when their forces arrived in Kabul from provinces, they were mobilized, armed and placed in certain areas. Rumors spread that there was a coup about to happen and the ruling party would slaughter people. In the meantime, the Kabul residents, who had begun to adhere to Islamic law and hijab above all, made a great deal of small speculations by promoting and spreading it. It was told to the public that upon Mujahidin's arrival, schools and universities would be closed and women and girls would no longer continue to work or get an education. Therefore, young girls were careful of their behaviours and regarded the Islamic hijab as appropriate. Additionally, families were not allowing their female members to go out fearing the circumstances.

Governmental employees were in a confusing situation about their employment status. Meanwhile, people had been trying to get membership in one of the Jihadi parties. Besides, there were groups of Mujahidin soldiers coming to Kabul and were placedin certainlocations. It was also impossible to prevent the Mujahidin soldiers from coming into the city with weapons. Kabul city was in the course of change because a large number of the Mujahidin had a different and strange style of clothing—long-haired, kohl-eyed, along with their trousers' legs pulled up—which made it unbearable to look at the city anymore. A completely new brand group of humankind replacing people in the most civilized city in the country.
Right on those days and nights, they opened the gates of the famous Pul-e-Charkhy Prison and all prisoners including political, criminal, and ethical were released. Yet, the presidential palace had not collapsed, and the members of the Watan Party, which belonged to Najibullah, were naming s Najibullah's unsuccessful attempt to escape as a cowardly act and therefore cursing him. However, the rumours were saying that the presidential palace was handed over to the Islamic Party's forces by General Rafi and he made way for 1,250 soldiers of this party to enter the palace through the eastern gate.

The Mujahidin were gradually coming to Kabul. First of all, the rumours were about mujahidin of the Islamic Unity of Afghanistan Party entering Kabul. I witnessed them preaching their goals and ideals in the Writers Association of Afghanistan; a representative of the party had come to the association and was talking to the editor of the newspaper. According to them, they had already captured several western parts of Kabul, like "Mirwais Maidan", "Karta-e-Se", "Karta-e-Chahar", "Kabul University "Bagh-e-Balla", and "Karta-e-Parwan". They had also captured some of the northern and central parts of Kabul, like "Taimany" and "Chendawol".

But the Mujahidin of the Ahmad Shah Masoud's Party, (Jami-at-e-Islami), had taken Afghanistan's National Television Network, some parts of the "Makrorayan Buildings", which are located in the north and centre of Kabul, and "Khairkhana", which is located in the north of Kabul city. They said that the remaining forces were located in the south of Kabul, and the Kabul Airport was captured by the forces of Abdul Rashid Dustom, who had remained an ally with Ahmad Shah Masoud back then.

In the meantime, some southern and southeastern parts of Kabul, like "De Khudaidad", "Qala-e-Zaman Khan", "Zamborak Mountain", and "Fifth Directorate of secret service agency", were controlled by the Islamic Party's forces led by Gulbuddin Hekmatyar, who had now allied with "Jabar, the Godless"." The mujahidin forces belonging to the Islamic Unity Party had captured some government offices and were now controlling the Shahr-e-New/New City" areas. With this, Kabul was divided between several congruent and heterogeneous divisions before the absolute collapse of the regime.

As far as I witnessed, Kabul's security forces had not yet completely dissolved because some of the remaining didn't leave and began to oppose the Islamic Party Mujahidin forces, but the war between them had not yet escalated. On the contrary, theft and spoliation were increasing day by day; whoever was in charge of an area would take anything he wanted from that area. The majority of youths who were jobless would go to the captured areas in Kabul, request weapons, and join the mujahidin; they let their beards grow long, wore Afghan local dress, and plundered the people. In addition, one of the scholars of the communist regime, who had spent his whole life translating communist and Leninist books and articles and was a major member of the Science Academy of Afghanistan, had now forced himself into being a "Mullah" after the Mujahidin governed in Kabul, publishing his articles with the prefix as "Mullah or Mawlana". This was how things were radically changing.

◆

But I can never forget the night when the Kabul regime collapsed. I had never spent a night as heavy as that. The night started with Mujahidin celebrating their triumph along with gun and air RPG firings that landed on the houses in Kabul. The rest of the night felt as if Kabul was breathing fast, like time bobs before an explosion. The next morning, due to the disagreement between Ahmad Shah Masoud and Hekmatyar, their forces started counter-attacking and fighting to gain each other's areas, but some of the rebellions, who had no place before and now were present in the city, abused the fight and took control.

Masoud himself had not yet come to Kabul, but the fighting had already taken place around the Presidential Palace, the Seventh Directorate of Secret Service, Makrorayan Gas Station, and the Interior Ministry.

The Interior Ministry had already been controlled by the Islamic Party of Afghanistan, and the rumours were that the party wanted to take over the government of Afghanistan and start a single-party system. Masoud's denial not to enter Kabul city was justified by the disagreement between him and Hekmatyar on forming a joint government.

The war between the Kabul Security Forces and the Islamic Party was still going on in southern areas of Kabul such as "Chaman-e-Huzuri" and towards end of "Maiwand Road", and rumours were saying that Shahnawaz Tanai and Watan-

33   The Beginning of an End

jar, two former Defense Ministers of Afghanistan, were leading the regime's forces against Mujahidin in "Shah Shaheed" and "Rahman Meena" areas in Kabul.

Two days before Masoud's arrival in Kabul, the Interior Ministry of Afghanistan was captured by Masoud's forces and entrusted to the Islamic Unity Party's men. The next day, they captured the presidential palace and it's surrounding areas such as "Shash Darak", "Mahmad Khan Bridge", and the seventh directorate of the secret service. One night before Ahmad Shah Masoud's arrival, the Afghanistan National Television Channel, which had been captured by Masoud's fighters, broadcast news saying that Gulbuddin Hekmatyar was about to stage a coup. However, the Islamic Party's radio channel also announced that it was Ahmad Shah Masoud's forces who committed the coup and overtook power. However, with the Nazar Council's dominance, the war was pushed back from the central areas of Kabul to Old Makrorayan, Dehkhudaidad, Qala-e-Zaman Khan, Qalacha, and Shahshahid areas and the missile fire from Zamborakshah Mountian was directed to the city.

According to the claims made by the Nazar Council, the coup of the Islamic Party was managed by and from the Ministry of Interior of Afghanistan. They would say that some of the members in charge of the failed coup were detained when the Ministry of Interior collapsed. Moreover, I have witnessed 12 Mujahidin belonging to the Islamic Party of Afghanistan being released after having been detained and disarmed in the Seventh Directorate of Secret Service. Many cases like that happened, but the people seemed to be critical of that, asking why would they release such militants.

Accordingly, the Nazar Council's fighters had now seized the presidential palace along with the Ministry of Interior of Afghanistan just one day before Ahmad Shah Masoud arrived in Kabul. More importantly, there were rumours that Ahmad Shah Masoud himself had been leading the fight from north of Kabul (Chamtala Deseret) and sought support from Abdul Rasheed Dustum's forces to overtake the presidential palace.

Generally, no other fraction was involved in the battle between Hekmatyar and Masoud's fighters. Other Mujahidin
parties called the war between the two parties and supported
neither of them.

According to Mohammad Sediq Barmak, an Afghan filmmak-
er and Director of the Afghan Film Industry, as soon as Ahmad Shah Masoud arrived in Kabul, he located himself in
Kabul's Security Forces Campus, where General Nabi Azimi,
a former minister of the Interior Ministry, was based. After
his military salute, General Nabi said to Masoud, "Glad you
arrived, Mr. Minister. arrival gives us morals and courage.
Then he showed the locations of their opponents in Kabul on
a map to Masoud. Later, Masoud mockingly replied, "Their
military generals were not clever enough. Otherwise, they
would not have been defeated despite their control all over
Kabul." Ahmad Shah Masoud was now selected as the Minister of Interior based on the agreements achieved among
Jihadi factions in Peshawar, Pakistan.

◆

 Anyway, those fighters who were not busy fighting during
those days began remarkable looting. First, they took whatever private and government vehicles they could and distributed them amongst themselves as if they were their own. On
the second run, they took all governmental military fleets. It
was said that the "Siahsang Vehicle Regiment " with all its
military fleet and even public buses were being sent from the
"Charasyab" route to Pakistan by Mujahidinarmed forces. Additionally, it was said that some unarmed groups were coming to Kabul city for spoliation, and Hekmatyar had ordered
his fighters to bring the stolen vehicles back to their place,
capture the thieves, and investigate the theft. But something
that seemed true was that the governmental cars, lorries, and
public buses were being stolen from every corner of the city.
The so-called Islamic Government had not yet formally taken
over, and people hoped that the situation would change after
the interim president was selected.

The Interim Government and Other Stries

The Convoy of Pajero Riders and People's Ovation

The following day, Sebghatullah Mujadedi, the interim president, arrived in Kabul from the Jalalabad route after years of living as a refugee in Pakistan. He was accompanied by his chosen cabinet and a convoy of Pajeros and trucks loaded with wheat, flour, split peas, and oil. The people, who had suffered from theft and robbery, welcomed their interim president with historic enthusiasm, lining both sides of the road and applauding his arrival. That afternoon, as he arrived in Kabul, gunfire from celebratory shots in the air resulted in thirteen deaths and forty-one injuries.

That night, the former government officials provided Mujadedi with the treaty of "fire and blood" (presidency) and left. Based on the Peshawar Treaty, the Prime Minister, the Minister of Defense, and the Minister of Interior had already been appointed. Later, the remaining ministers for Afghanistan's ministries were appointed based on each fraction's power rationality in the government. So they were called

37   The Beginning of an End

upon to run the government as usual. Accordingly, the mullahs in the mosques started to preachto people, and we realized that they were trying to teach and re-Muslimize us as if we did not know how to take ablution, go to prayers, etc. They were even close to making the Muslim couples remarry in the country to fit them into their way of being Muslim.

In his first speech in Pul-e-Kheshti Musque in central Kabul, the interim president began to read Hadith and Verses of Qoran and speak Arabic; he "thanked" people in the mosque in English (, There were rumours that the interim president has citizenship of Denmark, and plenty of his ministers have citizenship or green cards from western countries and indications were in places that those rumours will turn in to reality one day.

◆

Shortly after, the walls and buildings in Kabul were filled with photos and posters of different Mujahidin leaders and commanders with people getting used to the Islamic Party's rockets targeting them. The conversation was about the images of leaders and commanders. Yes, one smiling, another not; one dressed in white, another in black; one with a gun on his shoulder, another with a gun in his hand; one with a henna-dyed beard, another with a black beard; one with glasses, another without. Each, in appearance, was a different embodiment of tyranny. However, the prices of food suddenly dropped, bringing a scent of hope to the people, and they took comfort in this matter. Unfortunately, this respite was shorter-lived than any other government's, and after the first week, prices began to climb again, reaching unbearable levels. Later, we realized that it was all a very petty tactic by the leader-makers across the border in Pakistan.

Instead, moving objects had appeared in the streets and markets of Kabul. These were groups of men with long hair and beards, with rolled-up sleeves and torn collars, wandering up and down. In their hands were either stolen swords from the city's antique shops or stolen hatchets from those stores.

They ostensibly enforced good and forbade evil, approaching
women and young girls with eyes bulging from their sockets
and making lewd comments.

Their cigarette papers were emptied of tobacco and filled
with hashish, which they smoked openly in public. I swear
they hadn't washed their faces for a month or set foot in a
mosque's prayer area. They had no interest in government
work, the opposition, or those sincere and holy mujahideen
whose love for God was the sole purpose of their jihad. They
were new creatures that came along with Mujahidin to dis-
honour the city and its people.
The Mujahidin commanders did worse: each commander in
charge of controlling an area thought that the whole area
was his. In Khair Khana, north of Kabul, some of the Mujahidin commanders distributed parklands to their men and
allowed them to build illegal houses in those areas, though
they had not received any permission or legal property documents from the municipalities. Their fighters also started
building houses. (Imagine! These illegal house-buildings ru-
ined the area where, based on the city's master plan there
were all public facilities planned.
These illegal housing practices provoked other commanders too. I witnessed that a commander called Dawood Shah
Khan, who was so called the military commander of a district
in Panjshir province, seized and distributed 112 acres of an
area that belonged to deserving people who had legal property documents in Khair Khana's 11th district in the north of
Kabul. The legal owners of those lands tried to reach everywhere they could, but no one heard them. The strange thing
was that those legal owners were threatened by Dawood
Shah Khan if they got close to their property.

This was how the legal property and its owners were treated, think of public properties, people's assets which had no
documents etc. Those men even struggled to own a donkey
before then, but now they owned brand-new cars and vehicles. We got used to it when we saw the leaders' daughters,
sons, sons-in-law, and grandsons driving the finest cars. We
thought that when they stole from the poor refugees (in Paki-

stan and neighbouring countries), others were not to blame for looting the poor and collapsed city of Kabul.

About some of the statesmen

One of the landholders of heaven, someone as if you say was representative of God on earth, was deputy minister in one of the ministries. According to one of his servants, he was getting the salary of a high-ranking general and was a poet and writer as well. He was bringing his children to his office every day to prevent them from disturbing others on the street.
He, whose mouth used to foam and his lips shiver while speaking, had ordered to his men that his speeches be recorded every night and broadcast by the Afghanistan National Television Network. Watching him every night would remind us of the preachers of hell, and we would pray for God not to let us see him every night on TV. He had reached his current position as one key figure of one of the fighting fractions, and during rocket firings in Kabul, his standing with both those who shot and those who were being shot. He would always attack innocent women in his speeches, and there were no women left who had not yet been blamed. The man who was his minister was one of the charlatans of the century, and history knows about it. His vocation expenses were coming from the ministry, and he carelessly spent them all without anyone's permission. They had left their real duties behind and were busy talking about women and the way women dress, although the women knew that in an Islamic Government, they should wear an Islamic Hijab. Again, they never left women alone and spent their time talking and gossiping about them, whose brothers and husbands were either killed or they were caretakers of their sick family members.

◆

In a gathering of ministry officials and employees, a minister harshly criticized both men and women. He remarked, "Those whose wives work in offices and outside the home are dishonourable and without dignity." A young female engineer stood up in the same assembly and replied, "The dishonourable and undignified ones are those who are here while their wives and daughters are selling their dignity in foreign markets." This was indeed the situation of the minister. It is said that the minister told the girl, "If it weren't forbidden in Islam to hit a woman, I would have dealt with you. Now, don't let me see you in this ministry again." And it is said that the woman left the gathering with such pride that the minister was trembling with rage on his chair. The minister was the one who once asked women whether or not their growing nails would hurt their bodies during ablution. He had also asked girls and women why they did not marry their Mujahidin fighters, whereas all of them, including the Mujahidin fighters, were young. In the same conversation, a young woman stood up and replied that the minister should ask the first question from his family members first, and the second question, she said that educated women (doctors, engineers) would marry human beings, not animals.

The same minister one day asked his female employees to come to his office, put a bundle of cash in front of them, and said, "Each of you must pick whatever you need and buy a scarf for yourselves". The women replied: that traditionally, our fathers and brothers are supposed to pay for the scarf or clothing of the female family members and that they don't need the minister's money and left the office immediately.

◆

Another example of these times was the bodyguard or special guard of the interim president, who stood right behind him everywhere with an unusually tall stature, long beard, and bulging eyes as if the president himself were Napoleon, the conqueror of Egypt. He argued daily with the employees of the national television station about why his full-length image was not shown, unaware that the issue was not with the employees but with his unusual physique.

Eyewitnesses said that wherever the interim president went, this special guard would go there first and lie down on the carpets, sofas, and chairs to ensure that if a bomb or mine had been planted for the president, he would take the blow instead. He was unaware that, as the people of Kabul would say, they had no such intentions against government officials. Instead, they made jokes and funny stories about them and their associates. For instance, the people of Kabul had given this bodyguard a humorous nickname, just as they had given a mocking name to the special guard of the previous president. The people of Kabul used their humour to make their points to the officials, many of whom did not understand.

What happened in Afghanistan's National Radio Television Network?

One day after the Mujahidin came to Kabul, Afghan instrumental players and singers, who had already sung revolutionary songs for the previous regimes, started to sing for the victory of the Mujahidin and the Islamic revolution. It's interesting that among the people of the arts, this group was the most opportunistic (although perhaps their profession demanded it). Later, when the civil war started, these singers went to several fighting fronts, and each one sang songs for a particular fraction, and that's how they secured their income. The same scenario happened to the writers who wrote for the previous regimes, and, after April 28, 1992, they became admirers of the Mujahidin suddenly.

Subsequently, music was banned from the radio and national television networks, and artists, young and old, were the first ones to leave Kabul. Some of them went to Mazar-e-Sharif, the northern province of Afghanistan; some others migrated to Pakistan, Uzbekistan, and Russia, which means that the musicians were among the first group of people who became vulnerable after the regime changed and the Mujahidin took power.

◆

Censorship was another issue that started within the Afghanistan National Radio and Television Network. It was so extreme that they cut a scene in which the rat was dancing, and, in another cartoon, they didn't allow a scene in which a female pig was walking on the beach. In the animal documentaries, they censored scenes in which the birds got together and kissed. In cinemas, in the middle of movies, some particular scenes are cut or only the pictures go dark but the sound only continues for minutes or seconds though the audience can hear the sound but can't watch the scene. With all these restrictions, radio and television staff were threatened constantly by some of the leaders.

◆

Another case that sparked anger among people was that female presenters and journalist were banned from presenting and appearing on the screen and raida programs. The leader of a Mujahiddin fraction once said to the two members of a board—one of them was from the Shia Sect and another had been educated in the U.S.—that "I do not recognize any person from the Shia Sect, and you, who have been educated in the U.S., are a U.S. citizen, and I do not want to talk to a U.S. citizen!" One of the leaders of another fraction had told a group of journalists that he felt ashamed whenever a female anchor called his name (in the news or on TV programs).

◆

Another disastrous thing that happened in the national radio and television was that they destroyed or stole the archives. Later, those who wanted to collect some documentary films from the archive got to know about it. The former director of military units of national radio and television was someone who was dubbed by the name Mirza Qalam, a pseudonym for his comedy character on the radio; after all, he knew everything about the archives including items, history, locations and of course methods of destroying them.

◆

But we also witnessed something that had never happened throughout the history of properties: the seizure of lands belonging to the Afghan Film and Radio Television government institution, which were marked and laid the foundation by one of the Jihadi ministers coming from Pakistan to build a personal house and property on it. Another matter, which is also related to radio and television, was the trend of creating generals. After the first speech of the interim president, the issuance of decrees and orders for promoting individuals to the rank of general began to be broadcast on the radio and television. Every night, a list of newly appointed generals, most of whom had come from Pakistan, was read out, and we witnessed a variety of generals in the city: military generals, civilian generals, armed generals, uniformed generals, non-uniformed generals, cleric generals, mullah generals, mounted generals, foot generals, abluted generals, non-abluted generals, ... and it got to the point where becoming a general became a topic of humour for the people of Kabul. Whenever they saw someone idle and unemployed, they would say he should go and become a general. After a while, the government stopped appointing generals, as if it had run out of generals. A friend of mine who worked in the ANRTN told me the story of this case. So, I added it based on my memory of his story:

"One day, Zabiullah, son of Sebghatullah Mujadedi, the interim president of Afghanistan, and one of the generals belonging to Abdul Rashid Dostum entered the ANRTN studio, carrying a long list of the newly appointed generals with themselves. They told the broadcasting manager that the list should be read after the news. So, the broadcast manager told them that Defense Minister Ahmad Shah Masoud had ordered that no order regarding general appointments be accepted or broadcasted without his signature (approval), and Zabiullah said that he wanted to talk on the telephone and coordinate with Masoud himself. So, after a short greeting on the phone, Masoud loudly said to the interim president's son, Zabullah, "What are you doing there at the ANRTN studios? What do you know about military service? Then, Zabiullah responded that the interim president, his father, had ordered him, but Masoud sparked with anger, told him to leave the studio immediately. Then, Zabilullah said, "Is it a coup?", and

Masoud responded with anger, shouting, "Yes! Tell your father too. Just leave the studio now; otherwise, I will order them to take you out of there with force!"
At this moment, General Majid backed off, and Zabiullah got out of the ANRTN news studio with a long list of newly appointed generals in his hand.

◆

In those strange days, the children adapted an old and popular song with new, critical, and protesting lyrics. Traditionally, the song is sung while the children form a circle, hold hands, sit down, and stand up. Now, they sang the song with these new, critical lyrics. Their Critical song was:

Quo quo quo, plane tree leaves,
Leaders sitting in rows,
Counting rupees and pounds,
Their work is killing and war.
I wish I were a leader,
Flying high in the air,
Drinking Zamzam water there.
I wish I were Sibghat,
In power, I'd sit flat.
I wish I were Rabbani,
In the seat of power, so fine.
I wish I were Sayyaf,
Under blankets, I'd lie and laugh.
I wish I were Gilani,
Counting dollars, so many.
Gulbuddin said, "Oh no, oh no,"
Massoud said, "Pain and woe."

Tales of looting and devastation
The looting of the Writers Association's Office

As I said before, the governmental and social buildings were invaded in the first days of the Mujahidin's seizure. The Writers Association's Office, where I used to work, was invaded by some militants belonging to someone so--called "Jelani," who declared that he belonged to the "Islamic Unity" fraction. Jelani was nothing more than a 25-year-old young man who was born in Shakar Darah, a district in the north of Kabul, and his group, which consisted of junkies (hashish addicts), would sit in the large garden of the association office, lighting their smokes full of hashish and planning thefts.

These people, who had fought for 14 years and called themselves pure Mujahids, stole everything from the office including carpets, kitchenware, tables, chairs, curtains, TVs, radio recorders, and telephones—from the association within one night after they raided the office. They didn't leave anything. The next morning, when I went to the association, they were taking some chairs—we used them for sitting in the garden

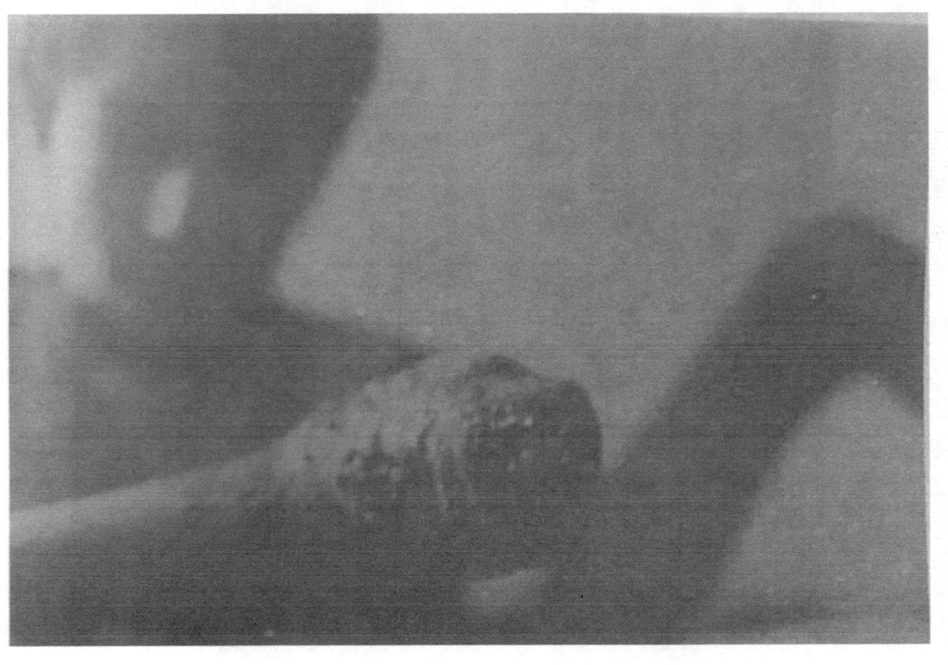

47   The Beginning of an End

to take a breath of fresh air—from the association's store-house and loading them in a truck to take them away. Some of those Mujahidin were helping the driver and his assistant to load it quickly. Jelani was sitting in the chair of the director of the association, smoking hashish.

Later, the association's staff arrived, and we all gathered in the corner of the garden and saw the librarian of the association, angry and saddened, coming toward us to say something. Then we realized that the whole library was emptied. We are doubtful, saying, So strange! What could Jelani do with books? But Jelani was still sitting on the director's chair, enjoying smoking hashish.

We had six vehicles, one of which was used by Jelani, and the five others were missing right after he and his men took control of the office. The weird thing was that they were still blaming us for our critical comments on what they were doing to the office and threatened that they would not leave any of us without punishment, but we remained clever enough: we kept calm, kept our heads down, and walked our way.

Later on, Jelani got calmer and treated some of the staff of the association well. He would say about the plundering, "Some other group had done it before they arrived. After he realized that he was making excuses, he would say, "Is not our 14-year-old Jihad worth it? We responded, "Yes. You didn't do anything. Your fight was very worthy.

Not surprisingly,, those Mujahidin were selling the cradle telephone systems on the street: each telephone cost 50.000 AFN. While bargaining a customer had told to the Mujahid soldier that the phone was worth more than 5,000 AFG. The soldier replied to him that if you bought it from the government, you have to pay 100,000 AFG. This is not just judgment. The poor Jihadi soldier didn't know that it is the license that is expensive while buying from the government, not the device.

Finally, Jelani's group left the association, and another

group came along. The leader of the new group was called "Sayed Hamid Agha", who declared that he belonged to the Jamyat-e-Islami Party. He and his group stayed in the association until the end. There was only one untouched bookstore in the association office which had important academic books, the new group loaded them in a car and took them to the town to sell. In addition, they even took everything that they could think of selling such as door hardware, water pumps for the garden, flour containers, and firewood. In the end, they cut the trees in the garden and sold the wood to the wood sellers.

In the gap between Jelani and Sayed Hamid Agha groups' control over the office, another group temporarily took over the association. They said that they belonged to the Nazar Council. There was nothing left for them to take away, or perhaps they didn't want to risk their reputation by taking low-value items away. They just took some novels and poetry collections published by the Writers' Association of Afghanistan. Indeed they asked permission which was granted.

However, we did not put hands over hands and a few times went to the relevant appointed security office and complained about what happened to our office. Sadly, later on, we realized that the thieves stole things in coordination with the police stations: they stole people's properties and robbed shops at night. The burglary of the Afghanistan Writers Association was the darkest memory that still hurts me a lot.

The collapse of Khost Province and the metal trade

Even though this case has nothing to do directly with events in Kabul, it has much relevance, in terms of the method of burglaries that happened in Kabul.

Khost, the southern province of Afghanistan, neighbouring Pakistan, was the first province that collapsed in the hands of the Mujahidin before Kabul; there were so many abnormalities in Khost, including the burglary of governmental offices and treasuries at the hands of Mujahidin commanders. One of the goods exported from this province Pakistan was inactive ironworks, which were being found by Mujahiddin here and there. It was so strange that the buyers on the other side of the borderline (Pakistani traders) were not buying the military fleet and ammunition including tanks, humvees, military cannons, warships, and civilian aircraft etc. Instead they wanted them as only useless ironworks. That is why the commanders would primarily destroy the military tanks and aircraft with bombs and later sell them as kilograms of ironwork. This was as if there well thought plan for the demolition of Afghanistan's military, its properties and warcraft.

Finally, the commanders even wrapped up the metal carpets of the emergency airport in Khost province and sold them, and people began to call them ironmongers. Later on, such cases happened a lot after the collapse of Paktya province and Kabul, where they acted so extremely that they took out power cables of electro-motors and sold them as copper in kilograms in Pakistan. This happened a lot in the factories. (The commanders did not even know that if they didn't separate the power cables from the electro-motors, the electro-motors themselves would have been much more expensive than their cables.)

The only thing that Russians left in Afghanistan was millions of tons of iron and alloy steel, which could have been an important economic good and used in the construction of Afghanistan if they were not destroyed, but the Mujahidin commanders exported and sold them at cheap prices in other countries. (The metal trade had not yet happened in Kabul-Baghlan, Kabul-Panjshir, and Kabul-Parwan-Kapisa highways by the time as there were still the bodies of military fleet and warfare and irons pieces lying here and there along those highways).

It was reported that, on the Durand Line between Afghanistan and Pakistan, the smuggling of narcotic drugs was free, and, according to people, there were signs and boards in every shop that said "Best Heroine" or "Best Hashish". The shops that sell weapons smuggled from Afghanistan were open freely. Those weapons were sold at cheap prices by the

Mujahidin commanders! When the weapons are needed, the weapon sellers in the Durand Line (Pakistan) sell them to the Afghan Mujahidin fractions at very expensive costs to bring them back to Afghanistan. For instance, during the civil war, the fighting factions bought their weapons from that international market.

The stories of Ibrahim

Ibrahim is one of my friends, a Shia Muslim from Herat province in western Afghanistan, who was held hostage for a time by members of one of the Jihadi groups. He sold his house in Macrorayan 3, Kabul, and gave the money to the Jihadi captors to save his life. Then, as soon as possible, he left the country and became an immigrant forever. Ibrahim had stories and observations from his time in captivity that, when he recounted them to me, he couldn't hold back his tears, and his throat was constantly choked with emotion. What you read in this section are Ibrahim's firsthand accounts. He said that one day, the kidnappers brought a stylish Pashtun young man and told him to stand in the middle of the courtyard, a place where they kept the captives. The young man was trembling due to fear, though he was beaten on the way so hard that his mouth and nose were bleeding. His lips were dry and cracked, and there were drops of blood on his shirt. The kidnappers had taken out his shoes and his hands were tied behind his back. The kidnappers had circled the young man and were beating him hard (fists and kicks). The person in charge of the kidnappers turned his face to them and said, "Have you ever seen a chicken dance? The kidnappers asked, "What is a chicken dance? The commander said, "I will show you now". As the commander said, he got close to the young man, cut his throat's arteries with his knife, and backed off. The poor young man, gurgling and spinning in front of everyone, writhed in the dust and blood in his dying moments. Slowly, all his strength left him, and as if he were cradling his head, he finally became still.

Ibrahim continued, crying, saying that he didn't know why he thought of the young man's mother in those moments, wondering what she might have been thinking during those difficult times. He continued... Shortly after the young man had died, the commander asked the kidnappers, "Did you see what a chicken dance is like?", and everybody laughed and said, Yes." Wiping out his tears, Ibrahim added that the young man was martyred even more innocently than Husayn (the grandson of the prophet Mohammad), who was martyred in Karbala. Later, one kidnapper took the young man's hands, and the other two took his feet and threw him in the well in the courtyard (many innocent people might have been thrown in that well before). Then Mohammad, the commander, took a packet of cigarettes and asked others to take one too. Now, everyone lit a cigarette in their mouths and left the place.

◆

In another account, Ibrahim said that an old man, fearing the oppression of the Mujahideen, had moved his family and belongings elsewhere. When he returned home, the Mujahideen captured him and demanded ten million Afghanis for his release. They insisted that the money be brought by his daughter-in-law, with the intention that the commander of the captors, who was said to be attracted to her beauty, could assault her. Ibrahim said that the kidnappers brought the old man around noon, having tightened his hands behind his back. They had beaten up the old man a lot as it was apparent on the old man's face. Again, they made the old man stand in the middle of the yard and and beat him so much that he was lying on the surface. At their commander's order, the kidnappers pissed on the old man's face. Then, it was the commander's turn; he came close, kicked the old man's face, and said, "Open your mouth! The old man could not open his mouth, looking innocently at the commander, but the commander pissed on his face, eyes, and beard and said, "You wanted to keep them (the hidden stuff) away from me, huh? Later, the old man was taken to Ibrahim's cell, where he went through hard sicknesses. He had a high temperature. Three days later, one of the kidnappers came and took the old man away from the cell, and Ibrahim didn't know what happened to him.

◆

Moreover, Ibrahim told a story he had heard from a man who was in the same cell with him: during the civil war, a fraction captured a soldier from the opponent fraction. The captivating soldiers wanted to take the captive and threw him into a Mudbrick kiln. The captive belonged to the Payluch Group (a group of people who believed in bravery and manly behaviours and resided in the Kandahar province of Afghanistan. Meanwhile super loyal to his relevant Mujahidin leader). As the kidnappers were planning to take him to the brick kiln on the way, the captive began to curse the kidnappers, as they told him that they wanted to burn him aliv e After the captive had heard it, he said that if the kidnappers were no cowards, they should leave him to throw himself in the brick kiln stove by himself. The kidnappers didn't believe in him at first but later released him. So he spotted the face of the kidnappers, kept walking with a broken leg, and threw himself into the burning brick kiln.

Insulting women

No woman in the history of humankind has ever experienced what women and girls went through in Afghanistan after Mujahidin's victory. I would like to tell two of those horrible stories of women and girls in the aftermath of Mujahidin.

◆

They say that in one of the areas around Kabul, a pregnant woman went into labour. Her husband took her out of the house to get her to a hospital and stood by the road, hoping to find a ride to take them to the city and the hospital. A vehicle with armed night patrols arrived at the spot and stopped when they saw the man and his wife. The husband, pleading and begging, asked them to take his sick wife to the city or a hospital. The gunmen agreed but instead of taking her to the hospital, they brought her to their checkpoint.

There, the gunmen called some of their comrades and asked if they had ever witnessed a woman giving birth. They said no. One of the men who had brought the woman said, "Come on, tonight we will see a woman giving birth." They all sat in a circle in the room, watching the woman who was writhing in pain, crying and wailing. They also tied the husband's hands and made him sit beside her.

As the night wore on, both the woman and the half-born baby died from the excruciating pain and suffering. Then, in a barbaric manner, they threw the husband and the dead bodies out of the checkpoint. They mocked the husband, who was silent with grief and anger, by mimicking his wife's cries of pain.

◆

A friend of mine who has been a military officer said that after conquering a building where he killed many of his opponents, he found a group of captives in which a young woman was included as well from the basement. He knew the reasons behind the captivation of the men as they were either for money or because of party disputes, but he could not figure out what the woman was doing amongst them; when she was asked, the woman had responded that 14 days ago, she was going to pay a visit to her husband's parents because her husband was missing, but she was taken by Mujahiddin men on the way and brought to this place. Since then, she was constantly raped every night by 10-14 Mujahidin soldiers.

The woman had three children, two sons and one daughter, and was a female school teacher, but now she had lost a lot of weight and was mourning and crying.

Attack on the Hindu (Sikh) Minority and their properties

Hindus are a small minority in Kabul. They never interfered in any politics, but, unfortunately, they witnessed and experienced things and incidences by Mujahidin men that nobody had seen before. Sometimes, they were rarely disturbed by some thieves before the so-called Islamic Revolution, but this time, what they experienced was under the flag of Islam and Jihad.

One night, a group of gunmen covered with face masks stormed the house of a Sikh in Kart-e-Parwan, where this minority group lives. They imprisoned the entire family in one of the basement of the house. Then they collect all the stuff belonging to the family including jewellery, cash, clothes, furniture and supplies and load them in a truck that they brought for this purpose. The father of the family, who was socially respected and had a reputation in his community, had preferred to keep silent in order to not make inform the neighbours as he had adult daughters expecting the mujahidin soldiers to be satisfied with what they take from his house. But the   cowardly soldiers raped his daughter in front of his eyes and his family

At this point, the man started to shout out loud and ask for help, but nobody came to help him and his family due to fear. Finally, the armed men killed the father, injured his wife, and left the house as if nothing had happened in the neighbourhood.

◆

Another Hindu citizen was taken by Mujahidin men after they loaded his entire life's property and stuff from his home in a truck to ensure that he would not create problems after they left the neighbourhood. Once they unloaded the truck in their safe house, they left the man in the middle of nowhere. Eventually, the poor Hindu was taken away by another group of Mujahidin men. After a month, when the kidnappers were paid money, the poor man was released.

◆

Many cases like those happened to the Hindu minority in Kabul. For instance, a Hindu trader was beaten to death by the armed Mujahidin men in public to get to know where the Hindu man had kept his dollars safe. The man was dead after a week. In short, everyone has done something bad to the Hindu minority.

My observations

Some days after the conquest of Mujahidin, we heard a noise from the fourth floor of the neighbouring block's apartments in Makroraryan. It was afternoon, and we went and saw that a woman had been beheaded. When asked about the murder, the neighbours said two (or three) strangers got into her apartment and left immediately. All that the woman could do after her throat was cut was drag herself to her apartment's exit door to keep the neighbours aware by knocking on the door. Then she died. According to the witnesses and neighbours, she had been an agent of the former Afghan communist regime's secret service "KHAD". So, working there, she had found enemies, and now her enemies had the chance to kill her.

The woman had a little daughter. Then the governmental police stations began to search for her murderers, but after the rocket-firing escalated, everyone forgot about her.

◆

One day, around 8:30 in the morning, I left my home for my workplace through Malek Asghar Avenue and the Foreign Ministry's road (both places are located in the centre of Kabul). At the bus stop in front of the Kabul Public Library, I passed by three men who were wearing formal suits (after the revolution, only governmental workers were allowed to wear suits). As I wanted to turn to the Foreign Ministry's road, I saw that a white Volga stopped in front of me on the corner of the road. Three men got out of the Volga. All of them were wearing local Afghan clothes. Two of them were 19 or, perhaps, 18 years old, and the other was in his mid-twenties. The men stepped onto the pavement in a hurry and hid behind a metal booth that, in previous regimes, used to guard the roads leading to the foreign ministry, prime minister's office, and presidential palace. In the meantime, the youngest of the three was shivering due to fear, but the older one was encouraging him to be brave. I was paying close attention to the three men. Later, I felt that something bad and dangerous was going to happen. Still afraid, I turned a blind eye to them because I did not want to see the whole adventure. Other pedestrians did the same. Taking some steps forward, we heard a hidden, noisy dispute.

Looking back, I saw the first suit-wearing men being dragged by the other three who got out of the Volga, whose doors had been left open. They hauled them, and the suit-wearing men were still showing resistance. Therefore, I began to walk faster, so I was not to be involved in that adventure.

They were still in the fight when I heard gunfire, not once but three consecutive times. My whole body felt cold, and I realized something terrible had happened to somebody. Walking fast, I saw the noise made by the crowd who were escaping. Later, the car left, and it was clear that the car would accelerate and disappear from the area. After some moments, as the Volga passed by me, I began to feel alive and looked back and saw a crowd of people; meanwhile, I asked a pale-faced man who was passing by me, walking, about the accident. I said, "What happened? He responded, "They shot somebody". The guy who was killed was a famous person, which is why the story of his murder spread so fast among the government employees. We got to know about him soon: we heard that the man who was killed had worked with the communist regimes, working in the Ministry of Foreign Affairs and, once, as a governor.

◆

Another case that I witnessed happened on a video recorder cassette, which is not irrelevant to mention.One night, when my friends and I were watching an Indian movie, in the end, as we wanted to change the cassette, we saw that the movie had another ending too, which was about the civil war in Kabul (obviously, the Indian movie we watched was recorded on this film, but we did not know why).

The next five-minute-long film, on which the Indian movie was recorded, showed a jeep in which a driver and an armed man were sitting along with two other men who were wearing Afghani burqas (also known as chadaris). The fifth person was the cameraman himself, whose voice we could hear.

Driving on the rough roads and deserts, we finally watched as the jeep arrived in a desert. At that moment, we could hear the cameraman's voice saying, "These two men that you see are our captives who were trying to escape from the area wearing chadaris (Afghani burqas). Driving, the driver of the jeep asked the armed man, "Where to go? And the man responded, "To the brick-kiln". At this point, the short film ended.

◆

Once, I felt very ashamed. I was in a minibus, heading toward the centre of Kabul. A middle-aged woman got on the bus at a station. She was crying, cursing the Mujahidin, the Muslims! I realized that they had done something wrong to the poor woman, which was why she had been cursing them all along.

The poor woman was drying her eyes when she saw my face and recognized that I was Qahar Asi, the poet. She shouted at me, "You wrote your poems against the communists. So write about these faithless infidels too! I kept silent. At that moment, she got angrier and said out loud, "I am talking to you, Mr. Qahar Asi! Those thieves entered my house last night and stole everything I had. I kept silent again, showing that I was not Asi. I was looking outside when a man sitting beside me on the bus said to me, "The lady is talking to you! I responded, "Let her say whatever she wants to. Meanwhile, everyone on the bus started to look at me. Then, the woman said, "You said welcome (to the Mujahidin)! Welcome! Now, look at what they are doing."

I could not raise my head and kept silent. I learned a lesson that day but in a difficult way.

Some short but worth-reading tales

One day, a man on a bicycle was passing by a military check-point. Then, one of the armed men asked the cycling man to stop and said, "Do you want to buy a bicycle? The man on the bicycle replied, "I have this one. I do not need another one. The armed man said, "I was talking about your bicycle. You should buy it because it belongs to me now."
The man on the bicycle had to give the armed man whatever he had: a ring, a watch, and money. Later, the man could take his bicycle back from the armed man.

Bicycle theft was a simple practice that usually happened in front of military checkpoints. One was riding on a bicycle, and, suddenly, an armed man would stop him and say, "Brother, give me your bicycle", or "I have something to do up there; please give me your bicycle. I will bring it back to you". If one gave the bicycle away, it was gone forever! If one did not give, the armed one would know how to take or steal it from him.
One day, my brother's bicycle was taken away by the guards of the Kabul Governor's Office. My brother, who was a serious man, complained about the guards to the governor himself, bringing eyewitnesses too. The governor had told my brother to come next week—perhaps he wanted to calm my brother down to take his complaint back—but, after my brother went back after a week, he was beaten up by the governor and his guards again, and they threatened my brother to put him in jail (that was how a governor threatened ordinary people. You can imagine the rest.)

◆

According to the witnesses, after the interim presidency of Sebghatullah Mujadedi, everything in the presidential palace was loaded in large trucks and taken with him as if he were his private renting house to another. Some said that a multi-million-dollars check which was aided by one of the foreign presidents to the people of Afghanistan also went missing as the interim president left the office.

◆

Another thing that happened in that period was that the ceremonial motorcycles were missing from the Terrific Office in Kabul. Those motorcycles were used to escort high-ranking officials. A friend of mine who had recently come from Kuwaita Pakistan said: "Some of those motorcycles were sold in the Kuwaita markets, and, for the advertisement, they had written boldly on each of them "Afghan Escort.""

◆

Once, I saw an armed man dragging a deer from Kabul Zoo with a rope he had tightened around the neck. He was certainly hauling the deer to his checkpoint to roast and eat.

◆

One of my friends travelled abroad with one of the Jihadi ministers. In the currency exchange markets of Peshawar, he witnessed that the minister secretly sold a $250,000 check, which was a donation from a foreign benefactor to the people of Afghanistan, for half its value.

There was an old woman who had attended a wedding at which I was present too, and she was saying she prayed for the unity and alliance of Muslims in Kabul. And she has spent nights and days crying and praying for unity to come into the country, but after the Mujahidin took power in Kabul, "Unity", and "Alliance" parties came along too! We prayed for God, and he gave us what we asked for. Now, we had to tolerate the situation.

◆

In the early days of victory and rocket firing in Kabul, there was a group that stole passengers' belongings in the Hood Khail neighbourhood. After they had stolen things from people, they used to ask them to repeat a slogan with them. The slogan was "Death to Mujahidin! Death to non-Mujahidin! Long live theft!"

●

One day a couple was walking with their little kid by a military checkpoint, and an armed man asked to stop. They stopped as soon as they heard the voice. The armed man carrying a plastic bag got close to the couple and said, Look!" We are not thieves. So, give us all your money and take this bag full of dried yoghurt. The poor man had no money, but he searched his pockets out of fear. He found 11,000 AFG. The armed man took the money, handed the bag to the couple, and said, "Take this and never say we are thieves. You paid us and bought it"

The couple left the area; as they reached their home, they found out they did not have anything to cook. So they thought that they could eat whatt was in the bag. They opened the bag and realized that there was something hidden at the bottom of the bag. Yes, there were 1,700,000 AFG in the bag, which some other poor people had already hidden from the armed men. The thieves had taken the bag without analyzing what was in it. So, They sold it to this couple.

The End

Indeed, they (the Mujahidin) made Kabul collapse along with its entire identity such as culture, ethics, infrastructures public services, etc as nothing could replace Kabuli ethics (despite communists' presence). What they (the Mujahidin) did in Kabul was banality, petrification, and Peshawarism.

Kabul was made to collapse in the marshes, which I mentioned, but no one prevented the murderers. These men lived their lives comfortably, like Karmal and Najibullah and their families; it was ordinary people who got killed.

The leaders of previous governments (who weren't even Muslims), despite all their scandals, at least stayed with the people. They would, albeit with much audacity and pretence, sit on the mourning mat with the people and even mobilize forces to defend their government. Sometimes, with just one call, they would don military uniforms and head to the front lines. But now, after the victory, those who would be the first to flee to Peshawar and Islamabad at the slightest skirmish had become the ministers and officials of the country.

Yes, Kabul fell, but Najibullah's predictions came true. What we, the people of Kabul, witnessed from those who claimed to be Muslims, we had never seen from any infidel, communist, or secret service member. They would never seize government land for personal homes, and we never saw any of them engaging in the smuggling of government weapons and ammunition. But with our own eyes, we saw how the claimants of Islam marked and claimed the lands of the people and the government, or sold piles and piles of weapons abroad.

Kabul fell in this manner, and the claimants of tearing down the Berlin Wall built dozens of other strong walls in the small city of Kabul. Sectarian walls, religious walls, ethnic walls, linguistic walls, regional walls, and so on. Nails were driven into the heads of Muslims, Muslims were sawed in half, Muslims were burned in pieces, and Muslim women and girls were raped. But no one from anywhere could do anything or perhaps didn't want to do anything.

◆

One of the activities after the Islamic revolution in Afghanistan was that the Islamic government punished them after their criminal files were complete—they were executed in the Zarnigar Park in central Kabul (international radio stations also talked about those executions very much), but, I thought, many people in power were passing time comfortably in Kabul; those were the ones who should have been executed in Kabul avenues without question. Talking about demonstrations and protests against atrocities in Kabul, those people used to say, "Since Kabul was the centre of corruption and immorality, what was going on in Kabul was predestined and less than what should have happened. Nobody said that nothing happened to the misusers and corrupts, but the poor citizens of Kabul are the ones who are and will be suffering and killed.

Among the activities of the government after the victory of the Mujahideen was the punishment of several non-Jihadi thieves and murderers who, after their cases were completed, were hanged in Zarnigar Park in Kabul. The international radio also made a lot of noise about the execution of these individuals, especially the manner of their execution. But in

65   The Beginning of an End

my opinion, those who should be hanged or stoned at the crossroads of Kabul first and foremost, without any trial or case file, are a bunch of foreign agents who sit safely in the centres of power in Kabul, indulging in luxury and pleasure. Some of them responded to the protests about what had happened to Kabul during this period by saying:

"Because Kabul was previously a centre of corruption and immorality, whatever befalls it is destined and still less than it deserves."
But no one said that the corrupt and opportunistic ones did not share in these sufferings; rather, it was the oppressed and poor people of Kabul who were trampled on, are being trampled on, and will continue to be trampled on.

Finally, it will not be irrelevant if a book written by a poet ends with a poem. In the end, I present this poem to a dear friend of mine who is a singer-songwriter who lives abroad. I wrote this poem to him after the Mujahidin came to Kabul he migrated.

Silent, Sir!

Speak not of music and mysticism, sir
Don't mingle much with the whirling dervishes, sir!
Silent, sir!
Refrain from bringing forth your voice as a ghazal from the
lute's throat,
Go bury your tambour and flute
In the memories of the soil.
Lest the blade of ex-communication from these vile and hol-
low gods
Fall upon your brow!
Beat the drum and shake your hands!
Accept your sorrow and your joy.
With mourning,
For happiness is not found in the lexicon of these times, and
you,
Don't heed it, sir!
Silent, sir!
Time holds a different measure now,
And it seems from the lute and lyre, the scent of heresy arises,
And it seems that all these makers of celestial music are in-
fidels,
Heavenly!

(Maulana, Hafez, and Bedil)
Go and bring your beloved dervishes
To the tavern that looks towards the promised East,
To dance!
With feet stomping and hands clapping,
They cast away the filth of dark creeds everywhere,
In this place, strive less for the music of love, sir!
Silent, sir!
Do you not see that man is now shaped by guns,
Not by the crafting of metaphors and passion?
Why, in search of your naive followers,
Do you blow these trumpets so loudly, sir?
Silent, sir!
Silent, sir!